C000319805

Peter Fincham has worked in most of the great hotels in [...] up being a sneak thief he has devoted himself to food. H[...] has consistently been voted Restaurant of the Year by [...] which he is the editor. Very keen on gardening, he grow[...] peas, beans, potatoes and wheat. Also keeps a small herd of sheep and goats. No mean feat as he only has a window box. In his own cooking Peter tries to combine the best of traditional English methods with the classic style of the great French chefs, allied with the exciting new range of flavours from India and beyond. He usually features Bird's Dream Topping.

Ian Moore (MA) is the world-famous author of *The G-Plan Diet*, a revolutionary new regime based entirely on eating three-piece suites. His other publications include *The More You Diet the Fatter You Get*, *Lose Weight by Overeating* and *Nonsensical Titles Sell Books*. Outside food his main interests are music and the countryside. He is in his late thirties and would like ideally to meet a sensitive, younger partner with a lively sense of humour, Dallas-style good looks and a lot of money. Box no. 493.

Dr P. R. McGrath is a nutritionist. He studied epidemiology at Queen Anne College, Luton, before spending two years in the United States researching coronary prevention. He returned suffering from stress and since then has led a hand-to-mouth existence, having sold all his cutlery. Dr McGrath is a family man — he has a wife and three children, all belonging to his next-door neighbour Mr Bennett the accountant. His hobbies include gardening, cricket and building six-foot high walls to keep the enraged Mr Bennett out. Over the years Dr McGrath has made a fortune from writing about food, but he's of such a neurotic disposition that he keeps it all in a top-secret safe deposit compartment at Victoria Station. Box no. 215.

'Blow wind, and crack your cheeks! Rage! Blow!'
King Lear III.ii.1

Shakespeare on the effects of a high-fibre diet · · ·

Illustrated by Nigel Paige

Food
MADE SILLY

Dr P. R. McGrath, Peter Fincham and Ian Moore

CENTURY · LONDON

Design/Gwyn Lewis
Graphics/Ian Sandom

First published in Great Britain in 1985
by Century Hutchinson Ltd, Brookmount House,
62–65 Chandos Place, Covent Garden, London WC2N 4NW

ISBN 0 7126 1021 9

Typeset by Deltatype, Ellesmere Port
Printed in Great Britain in 1985 by
Hazell, Watson & Viney Ltd, Aylesbury, Bucks

Foreword

Breakfast TV personality Frank Biff writes:

It's always a pleasure to be asked to write a Foreword for a book on the subject of golf/pets/holidays★, especially when the proceeds are going to charity, or indeed when they're not — as in this case. I can assure you that this is something that has always played a major role in my life, and many's the laugh I've had playing/doing/enjoying★ whatever it is.

A lot of people come up to me in the street and say, 'You're a lucky sod, aren't you?' and I say 'I'm glad you enjoy the show — keep watching!'

This is an entertaining and informative book, and I'm looking forward to reading it. As I say, life for me would be unimaginable without nice little jobs like this, which you can knock off in five minutes over lunch.

Invoice enclosed.

Frank

★delete as necessary

Early man had no traditions . . . early man was alone. Why? Why was early man alone? Because . . . he was early. Nobody else had arrived. Imagine this poor Stone Age creature staring into a glass of wine . . . nervously dipping into the Twiglets . . . desperately hoping someone else would turn up.

Eventually our ape-like forebears (or bear-like foreapes) discovered sex (see *Sex Made Silly*), and there was a great expansion of the population, caused by a pre-historic mating system called 'carbon-dating'.

After sex their thoughts turned to food, and the growing numbers of men and women began to notice the herds of pre-historic deer, antelopes, oxen etc. that roamed around feeling smug because nobody had yet devised a way of catching them. The problem was simple enough — man was never quick enough to trap any of these animals on foot.

So in desperation he invented weapons like spears, slings and bows and arrows.

This fact is often used by vegetarians (see *Cranks*) to prove that eating meat was the original cause of war. But they forget that before spears and slings man used to fight with carrots, avocados and hazelnut-rissoles.

Food in History

It is almost impossible to overestimate the importance of food in history, but we'll have a go:

'Food is of greater significance than all other aspects of history put together.'

There.

Food Today

So much for food in history: what about the role of food in the modern world?

It is a well-known fact that, at any given moment, two-thirds of the world's population is starving.

Starvation has many causes: war, drought, over-population, waiters having too many tables to cover and so on.

It is also well known that in Europe and America too much food is produced. In fact the EEC's main function seems to be the creation of useless stockpiles — butter mountains, wine lakes and rich farmers.

Some simple folk have suggested that a way of solving the problem of people starving to death in the Third World and at the same time getting rid of the excess in the West would be to send all the unwanted food to the starving millions.

This would be all right in practice but just does not work in theory.

Complicated folk who understand these things better realise that just giving masses of food to starving people would do them no good in the long run (though it might stop them dying in the short run).

The solution to these problems, they say, lies in capital investment programmes, intensive study and radical improvements to things like infrastructure.

Anyway, it certainly must involve plenty of people on research grants and UN salaries going to Africa and Asia, having three or four servants and driving around in Land Rovers.

Well it must do, or they wouldn't do it, would they?

Food and Health

Over the years food has been divided into categories in a number of ways, such as:

(i) Fat, protein and carbohydrate
(ii) Breakfast, lunch and dinner
(iii) Meat and two veg.

For the most part these traditional divisions have been discarded, and we now have:

(a) Food which is fattening
(b) Food which gives you cancer
(c) Food which tastes nasty.

Of course certain types of hamburger manage to combine all three.

Most illnesses and diseases, if they are not blamed on smoking and drinking, are attributed to food. So the question must be asked, 'Why do we go on eating?' To which the short answer is, 'Because we'd be dead if we didn't.'

Are you fat, flabby, unfit, unhealthy and overweight?

Uuughh!

Well, one of the best things you can do is to pay a beautician and plastic surgeon a quarter of a million dollars to transform you into a perfect human specimen.

The principle is easy.

But, you may ask, 'Where do I get the 250,000 dollars?'

The Scarsdrivel Diet

The ingenious Dr Scarsdrivel, a leading American nutritionist, has got round this problem by making up a diet and writing a book about it.

The Scarsdrivel Diet is an all-protein, low-fat, high-carbohydrate, no-protein, high-fat, low-carbohydrate, all-food, no-milk, all-milk, average amounts of everything diet.

The advantage of this painfully strict regime is that you can eat anything you like . . . provided you only eat it when you like!

Alcohol should be strictly avoided, unless you want to get pleasantly pissed in order to forget about how flabby, unfit and overweight you are.

It's very easy to say 'I'll start tomorrow.'

Stop putting it off!

WRITE A BEST-SELLING BOOK ON DIETS *NOW*!!

Scarsdrivel Diet Easy-to-follow 7 day plan

MONDAY — Get letter from bank manager saying you're vastly overdrawn . . . spending too much money on fat lunches in posh restaurants . . . feel depressed . . . go out for fat lunch . . . go out for fat dinner . . . throw up.

(*Target weight*: 14st.00.)

TUESDAY — Decide to become a millionaire by writing bestselling book on diets . . . (You're the only one so far who hasn't) . . . Research eating habits over lunch.

(*Target weight*: 14st.07.)

WEDNESDAY — Lunch with publisher . . . write book on bus going home . . . (If you can get bus into the typewriter.)

(*Target weight*: 15st.00.)

THURSDAY — Become best-selling author . . . appear on book programme . . . go for lunch with Jeffrey Archer, Shirley Conran and the Indian bloke whose name no one can spell.

(*Target weight*: 16st.00.)

FRIDAY — Become an enigmatic recluse . . . (mainly to avoid having lunch with Jeffrey Archer and Shirley Conran) . . . look up spelling of Salman Rushtie (try to work out some anagrams).

(*Target weight*: 12st.00.)

SATURDAY   Move to Los Angeles for tax purposes . . . hire personal beautician . . . also masseuse, work-out supervisor, dance teacher, plastic surgeon and tennis coach . . . travel round colleges collecting honorary nutritionology doctorates.

(*Target weight*: 9st.00.)

SUNDAY   Lunch at Dudley Moore's pad . . . drop dead while jogging on Malibu beach.

(*Target weight*: 3st.00.)

Alternative diets

If you've experimented with all the conventional diets and got nowhere, here are a few alternative possibilities to consider:

THE DIET OF WORMS

A little known papal bull in the Middle Ages. The Diet of Worms was in fact ignored by nearly everybody, except for a number of clans in the highlands of Scotland (see *Glossary*: Haggis).

THE HUNGER STRIKE DIET

A highly effective diet which can be followed in three easy stages:

(1) Align yourself to an extreme political cause

(2) Get so worked up about it that you go on hunger strike

(3) Just before it's too late, cave in and start eating again.

RECIPE FOR HUNGER STRIKE DIET

Take three eggs.

Separate the yolks from the whites.

Put the yolks to one side (better still, throw them away — you will not be needing them later).

Beat the whites of the egg in a bowl with a handwhisk. (*Breathing deeply through the mouth while you are doing it*).

Throw away the egg whites.

If you're still hungry you may eat the egg-shells.

(N.B. You may be worried about the build-up of cholesterol in the arteries. If so, only use two eggs.)

Food Rotation

This confusing phenomenon (see also revolving tables in Chinese restaurants) is based on the perfectly simple principle that if something is good for you one day, it's bad for you the next.

The 'Food Made Silly Guide to Better Eating' (see page 34) should be able to answer all your questions on this point. But do remember that by the time you read this everything may have changed completely.

If in doubt consult your local GP and bear in mind that the following terms are more or less interchangeable:

good	bad
organic	unwashed
natural	more expensive
unrefined	more expensive still
free range	eggs laid on the day the battery was being recharged
no preservatives added	goes off quicker
farmhouse	made in a factory by robots with little bits of straw sticking out of their mouths

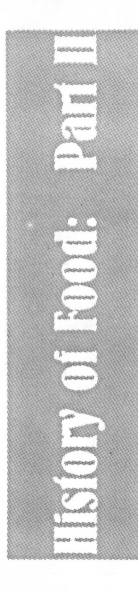

Modern man is descended from *Homo Sapiens*, the 'thinking man', so called to distinguish him from *Neanderthal Man*, a stupid, brute-like creature with a low forehead, hairy arms and what archeologists believe to be a Chelsea supporter's scarf.

In the early days cooking methods were simplicity itself, as the only surviving Stone Age Recipe demonstrates:

- Corner an animal (the bigger the better)
- Intimidate it with primitive grunting noises
- Slit its throat (or bash its brains out with rock)
- Hack it to bits with axe-heads
- Eat as much as you can before hyenas arrive
- Hand round the After-Eight mints

With the discovery of fire, social habits began to change. For the first time food could be burnt. For the first time when a man came home late after 'hunting bison' (Oh yeah, sure!), his wife could say 'What time do you call this? Your dinner's ruined!'

But man was still in the hunter-gatherer stage of his development. Animal husbandry was as yet unknown, with only one or two early men advanced enough to ask a sheep out for a drink.

The most important development of all — farming — still lay just round the corner.

When early man eventually crawled out of the glutinous fetid waters of the great primeval swamp, his first question must surely have been:

'Who the f*** pushed me in?'

The most important stage in his development came when he decided to become a farmer. Men realised that growing animals or plants on your own bit of land was easier than chasing around looking for them just as it was coming up to meal-time.

For one thing it saved time.

For another you could improve the quality of the things you were going to eat.

And eventually you would be able to attract a Common Market subsidy and afford a Range Rover and regular continental holidays.

Man enjoyed being a farmer, having long grown tired of running round after animals all day. So he bought himself a patch of land and settled down to cultivate it.

Times were good. With cultivation came grain . . . then wheat, corn, barley and oats . . . and of course bread . . . then someone suggested a ham sandwich, which meant running after those bloody animals again.

Hey!!! Here's a fantastic recipe for those all too often embarrassing moments when 5,000 Israelites turn up unexpectedly for dinner.

Fish Surprise

Fish Surprise — it's quick, it's cheap, it's miraculous!

The ingredients certainly shouldn't put too much of a strain on your pocket:

Five loaves (preferably unleavened)
Two fishes (get one of your apostles to fillet these; he won't mind in the least and otherwise it can be a messy and time-consuming chore).

Follow these simple steps and you can't go wrong:

(1) Take the five loaves and two fishes
(2) Give them to your disciples
(3) Disciples give them to the multitude.
If there's still not enough, beans on toast is always a good stand-by.

Next week: an inexpensive way of making your own wine.

Food Around the World

Below is a comprehensive survey of the cuisine of all major culinary nations of the world, based on thorough research carried out in as many as ten different restaurants in Soho, all within walking distance of our office.

French

France has often been described as the gourmet's Mecca. This is because gourmet's have a very poor sense of geography — Mecca is in fact in Saudi Arabia.

None the less, France is frequently said to have the best food in the world. Certainly this is the view of the French. Why this should be no one knows, except that they are quite an arrogant race and fiercely proud of their cuisine (kitchen).

In consequence all really good food in England is cooked by French chefs (chiefs) unless it is cooked by Indians (Indians).

A good many 'ordinary' English terms for foodstuffs were originally French words. So we don't order 'cow' at the butcher's — we ask for 'beef' (Fr. bœuf). The same is true for pigmeat, which we call pork (Fr. porc), sheepmeat (Fr. mouton) and veal (Fr. veau).

Even the word 'garage' is originally French. In fact we personally feel there is far too much French influence in the English language . . . but 'chacun à son goût'.

There are one or two characteristics of French cooking which may strike the foreigner as odd. For example, they

eat horses, don't they? In fact they even eat raw horsemeat on occasions. Indeed it is quite possible that jockeys in the longer horse races in France start nibbling away at their mounts as they gallop along.

Meat is but lightly cooked in France. A 'well done' steak to a French chef in France corresponds roughly to a 'medium rare' steak to a French chef in England.

A 'rare' steak is not only bloody in the middle, you can usually feel the pulse still beating.

And if you are brave enough to order a steak 'bleu' (blue) it ought, to be truly authentic, to be capable of the occasional moo.

Where to eat in France Same as in England, really — restaurants, hotels, bars, private houses if you're invited.

Spanish

Spanish food is nothing to write home about — which is why so many holidaymakers go there to save space on their postcards.

Italian

Italy is famous for its pasta which, like everything else, was actually invented in China. Marco Polo brought it back as a Chinese takeaway, since when it has settled down and made its home in Italy.

Types of pasta are named by the shape of object they happen to resemble, e.g.

Vermicelli = small worms
Spaghetti = A Birmingham motorway complex
Macaroni = Son of Aroni

Many Italian dishes consist of pasta topped with one of their unique and delicious sauces. A good example is Bolognaise sauce, named after any town in the world where you can mix mincemeat, onions, mushrooms and tomatoes together in a pan.

Tomatoes are of course not native to Italy, but were

'A La . . .'

Many people are confused by the French expression 'A la', meaning 'in the manner of . . .' (I'm not sure why: its meaning is pretty obvious). Here are a few of its culinary applications for the real dimwits among you:

- à la française . . . 'in the French way', i.e. in small expensive portions with too much garlic added.
- à l'italienne . . . cooked with too many tomatoes and a lot of superfluous hand movements and shouting.
- à la grecque . . . meat grilled on skewers and then served in a large wooden horse.
- à la chinoise . . . served in tin-foil containers and brown paper bags.
- à la suédoise . . . served with a turnip and an album by Abba.
- à la meunière . . . in the manner of the miller's wife . . . which is usually very quickly in the barn before the miller gets home (see G. Chaucer).

brought there from America by Marco H. Polo Jr.

Mincemeat isn't native to Italy either but is what most visiting forces have made out of the Italian army in the last few wars.

Scandinavian

A lot of people are of the opinion that Scandinavian food is among the most varied and exciting in the world. Well, I suppose they've got to believe something now that the Flat Earth Society has closed down.

After a promising start with a good deal of marauding, raping and pillaging, the Scandinavians have settled down to a wimpish and tedious lifestyle which is reflected in their cuisine (it would be reflected in their art and literature, but they haven't got any).

> **Norway** Famous for its unique open sandwiches (*Smørbrød*), the like of which are found nowhere else in the world.

> **Sweden** Famous for its unique open sandwiches (*Smörgåsbord*) the like of which are found nowhere else in the world.

> **Denmark** Famous for its unique open sandwiches (*Smørbrød*) the like of which are found nowhere else in the world.

But on the other hand the Danes do brew the most excellent lager . . . probably the best thing in the world to take your mind off those bloody open sandwiches.

German

The best food in Germany is the 'würst'. The worst food in Germany is a small spicy sausage.

The Germans also drink a strong lager called Somethingbräu which is lethal and two pints of it is enough to make anyone want to invade Poland.

Food Made Silly Map of the World

Fresian Cows

Icy Wastes

Baked Alaska

Turkish Delights (hashish, cocaine etc.)

Hungary

Swedes

Spuds

Starving

Back Garden of the Hamburger

Land of Milk and Honey (Tescos)

French Onion Soup

Black Forest Gateau

North China

Home of the Hamburger

Spanish Main Course

Breast of Turkey

Bone China

Caribbean Basin

Sahara Dessert

South China

Taiwan (Chinese Break-Away)

Prawn Madras

Coffee £14.95 + service

Heart of Africa

Kitchen Sink

Chicken Bombay

Prawn Caracas

Beer Gut of Africa

Pilau Rice

Sauce of the Nile

Mango Chutney

VAT Included

Roast Leg of Lama

Chilli Con Carne

Brazil (Where the Nuts Come From)

Paraguay (Where the Nazis Come From)

Nyasaland

Matabuliland

Pizzaland

Thousand Island Dressing

Horn of Africa

International Stores

New South Welsh Rarebit

Greek

If you want the best French food in the world, go to a peaceful village bistro in Brittany.

If you want the best Italian food in the world, go to a taverna piccola in the Tuscan foothills.

If you want the best Greek food in the world . . . go to Jim's Kebab House up by Haringey dog-track.

Travellers to the Hellenic isles have oft noticed how superior Greek food in England is to the real McCoy (or the real Dimitriou, as they call it).

Greek cuisine invariably consists of lamb, grilled on skewers and available in any shape or size you ask for (e.g. cubes, balls, ovals, misshapen lumps). This is usually served with a slice of lemon and some pitta bread, which looks like those padded envelopes used to send books through the post . . . and tastes like them by all accounts.

All this is washed down by a pine-flavoured lavatory cleaner called Retsina and a liquorice-based spirit called Ouzo, which is clear but turns cloudy when water is added and clear again if you add disinfectant (without altering the taste).

This is usually followed by a powdery, mud-coloured, sickly tasting coffee stolen from the Turks. The Turks, not surprisingly, didn't complain about the theft.

But to distract maximum attention away from the food the Greek waiters play bouzoukis and smash up the plates while you eat.

Indian

Excessive use of the sweaty clay oven, called a tandur, and heavy spices like cayenne and turmeric cause the furry red deposit on the walls of Indian restaurants.

But despite this and the endless piped George Harrison music, Indian restaurants remain popular because they give good value for money, the service is efficient and courteous and they are the only places likely to serve you if you roll up drunk long after the pubs have closed.

Ordering an Indian meal is an absorbing experience. You glance through the exotic dishes of the menu . . . think about trying a King Prawn Kashmiri . . . ponder over a Lamb Passanda . . . toy with the possibility of a Murgi Massola . . . then settle for the Chicken Madras you've had on the last fifteen occasions you ate at the same restaurant.

As a matter of fact you'd have probably done just as well with the Lamb Passanda. All Indian meals have roughly the same flavour, rather as all Indian Prime Ministers have roughly the same surname.

Kosher

The Hebrew/Yiddish word 'kosher' generally means 'fit to eat being ritually clean according to the Judaic dietary laws'. In an everyday sense this means meat from a four-footed, cloven-hoofed and cud-chewing animal, which is rendered dull, tasteless and leathery, i.e. quite unfit to eat. Other Jewish culinary terms include:

bagel a hard doughnut-shaped roll simmered in hot water for two minutes before baking then glazed with egg-white. An extremely easy form of exercise is to follow one of these around on foot in the hope of catching a hare. This is called 'bageling'.

latke a potato cake. The Yiddish expression 'flat vi en latke' means 'as flat as a pancake' or 'like a lead balloon' as in 'The bageling joke in the last entry was "flat vi en latke".'

lox   (sometimes loks, locks or lachs) smoked salmon with curls.

A friend of mine who is a Jewish Mormon from Salt Beef City works as a chef in a popular North London kosher restaurant. He tells this apocryphal tale from the Jewish culinary world.

A gentile asks a Jew why the Jews are so clever.

'Well, I'll tell you our secret,' replies the Jew. 'We Jews have discovered a certain fish which when eaten gives great wisdom and knowledge.' The gentile asks which fish it is. The Jew is at first reluctant.

'I cannot reveal such a secret to you, otherwise the gentiles will be as wise as we Jews. But I'll do one thing for you. I can give *you* a small piece of this fish that you may become wise, too. It will cost you, though. You will have to pay me £50 for this magic fish.'

The gentile agrees with alacrity. They arrange to meet in a certain seafood restaurant in north London the following day.

Next day . . . the gentile pays the Jew his £50 and is given a tiny portion of smoked haddock. He eats the fish in one speedy gulp, thinks for a moment then says, 'You know something? That fish tasted like a tatty old piece of smoked haddock!'

'But it was,' replied the Jew.

'I think it's a bit bloody steep! £50 for a bit of haddock!'

'Ah!' says the Jew. 'You see — it's already working!'

Terms of abuse In the international sphere, nicknames and terms of abuse for foreigners are often based on their strange eating habits.

The English call the French 'Frogs' because they eat snails, the German 'Krauts' because they eat cabbage (from Old High German: Hun . . . a cauliflower), and the Italians 'Wops' because they don't like them.

The Americans call the English 'Limeys' because they think we eat a lot of limes (which we don't), and the Australians call us 'Poms', which is said to be a shortened form of pomegranate — despite the fact that 90% of the population has never seen, let alone eaten, a shortened form of pomegranate.

In our grandparents' day (which in our house was the first Sunday of the month if Grandad could manage), you knew that something was good for you because your parents told you so. More recently, though, we have come to realise that our grandparents, although they lived without serious illness into their nineties, had incredibly unhealthy diets. Today, when we say that a certain food is good for us, we don't mean that it tastes nice, or even that it makes us feel better — what we mean is that we have read about it in some book called *Food and Health: The Facts*, or *Stuffing Yourself? Silly!*

It has become virtually impossible for the man or woman in the street to keep in touch with the latest theories regarding the links between food and health.

Pick up any paper and you will probably find that some American expert has published a book saying that something or other is bad for your health. (But be warned — picking up papers can cause serious skin irritations.)

The Scots are a good example.

They have one of the highest rates of heart failure in the world.

Is this because there are serious faults with the Scottish diet?

Or is it due to a succession of very bad goalkeepers in the international side in recent years?

Scientists can't agree — particularly American ones, who don't know the first thing about football.

Even if they were to agree, what exactly should be done about it? There are so many conflicting theories.

One day you read an article in the Sunday papers saying that it's now been decided that butter is better than margarine . . .

And the next day you hear someone on the radio saying that margarine should be preferred to butter.

One day a leaflet from the Butter Advisory Council pops through the letter-box pointing out how creamy and delicious butter is . . .

And the next day you bump into Leslie Crowther at the supermarket doing one of those bloody adverts for Stork.

Food is Bad for Your Health

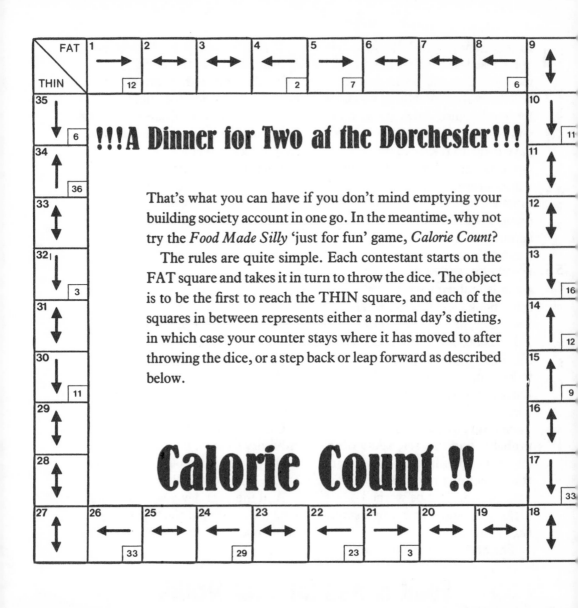

!!!A Dinner for Two at the Dorchester!!!

That's what you can have if you don't mind emptying your building society account in one go. In the meantime, why not try the *Food Made Silly* 'just for fun' game, *Calorie Count*?

The rules are quite simple. Each contestant starts on the FAT square and takes it in turn to throw the dice. The object is to be the first to reach the THIN square, and each of the squares in between represents either a normal day's dieting, in which case your counter stays where it has moved to after throwing the dice, or a step back or leap forward as described below.

Calorie Count !!

Calorie Count!! Key to Squares

1 You spend so long queuing in a fast food burger bar that by the time it's your turn, they've closed. Miss out on Big Mac and chips.

Lose 860 cal. Move forward — Square 12

4 You eat a bag of liquorice allsorts to take your mind off your diet.

840 cal. Move back — Square 2

5 Someone attacks you in the street and steals your Chinese takeaway. He eventually gets away after a 30-minute chase.

Lose 1,000 cal. Move forward — Square 7

8 A friend of yours who works in advertising invites you out for an expenses-paid lunch.

5,300 cal. Move back — Square 6

10 The escalators at Oxford Circus are broken so you have to walk up the emergency stairs.

Lose 620 cal. Move forward — Square 11

13 You accidentally glue your lips together. Can't eat for a week.

Lose 1,300 cal. Move forward — Square 16

14 You go on a low-fat, low-protein, high beer diet.

2,000 cal. Move back — Square 12

15 You dream you've eaten a giant marshmallow. When you wake up the pillow has gone.

150 cal. Move back — Square 9

17 You nearly get caught in bed with another man/woman's wife/husband. You have to hide in the wardrobe for 24 hours without food or drink.

Lose 630 cal. Move forward — Square 33

21 On the way home from a session at Weightwatchers you invite this man/woman you fancy out for a pizza.

750 cal. Move back — Square 3

22 One day you discover that you're so fat that none of last year's clothes fit. You decide to eat nothing all day except last year's clothes.

Lose 48 cal. Move forward — Square 23

24 You go to an expensive restaurant and eat an elaborate 5-course meal for two on your own. Then discover you have left your wallet at home. Go to gaol and live on bread and water for three months.

Lose 200 pounds. Move forward — Square 29

26 Julian and Caro invite you to dinner in Islington . . .
They've turned vegetarian and all you get is one stuffed
pepper and a soya-bean salad.

Lose 820 cal. Move forward — Square 33

30 The plane you're travelling in crashes in the Andes . . .
you end up having to eat your fat companion.

2400 cal. Move back — Square 8

32 The diet book you've written is so successful that
you're invited onto *The Observer* food tasting panel . . . the
first day you have to compare 43 different varieties of
cream gateaux.

1,000,000 cal. Move back — Square 3

34 You go on holiday to Morocco, develop gastro-
enteritis, and can't eat for a fortnight.

Lose 1,367 cal. Move forward — Square 36 (WIN ! !)

35 Having dieted conscientiously for six months in your
Balham bedsitter, you go home to your mother's for
Christmas. She says you're looking thin . . .

375 cal. Move back — Square 6

**NB You must throw the correct number on the dice to
land on the *THIN* and win the game.**

The Food Made Silly

Guide to Better Eating

Bread

It's been said that 'Man cannot live on bread alone' . . . though why it should make any difference who he's with while he's eating it is unclear.

Bread used to be classified as starchy and fattening, but lately it has enjoyed a revival. We each eat roughly 2lb of the stuff every week, although a lot of it is fed to the ducks. Of course there aren't as many ducks as there used to be, as a result of bread poisoning . . . hence the phrase 'Ducks cannot live on bread alone.'

Unsliced bread was once thought to be better for you than sliced, but it's now acknowledged to be more dangerous to your health. If you cut a loaf with a kitchen knife you risk cutting your finger. If you cut your finger you just might develop tetanus and lockjaw. If you develop lockjaw you'll probably starve to death.

Sliced bread, on the other hand, isn't dangerous at all — unless you put the plastic bag it comes in over your head and suffocate.

Salt

Salt basically comes from the sea — hence the expresson 'salt of the earth'.

Traditionally people used to sprinkle it indiscriminately over boiling vegetables, plates of chips and iced-up roads. This is now considered inadvisable for the roads, leading as it does to high blood pressure, irritability and hardening of the shoulder.

Various other superstitions appertain to salt, for instance that you need to increase your consumption of it during hot weather to avoid dizziness. In the old days, people travelling to tropical countries used to take a supply of salt tablets for this very reason. More recently, customs officials have got wise to these 'salt tablets' and they've become a criminal offence.

Throwing a pinch of salt over your shoulder is considered good luck — though it's bad luck for anyone standing behind you.

Fish

Fish of all sorts are good for you — after all, other fish eat almost nothing else.

When buying fish, be sure it's in good condition. If the eye is sunken, the flesh soft and the skin dry and gritty, it's probably stale and ought to be returned to the fishmonger. If the gills are shiny, the eye bright and it has a seaweedy smell, then it's fair to assume that it's fresh. If it caresses the inside of your thigh with its fin, then it's getting very fresh indeed and ought to be given a cold shower.

Sugar

Sugar was once thought of as a luxury, rather like caviar . . . though nicer tasting . . . I mean, you wouldn't want a spoonful of caviar in your tea, would you?

It would surprise most people to learn that they eat 20 times as much sugar as they did 200 years ago. Then again it isn't all that surprising — 200 years ago they weren't even born.

This increase in sugar consumption is sometimes regarded as an accidental by-product of food manufacturers trying to entice us to buy their products by making them sweeter and sweeter.

This is, of course, nonsense. The bastards are in fact trying to kill us. They're all in on it. Confectionery companies. Multinationals. Food canners, packers, driers. And governments. All the governments in the world are in the pocket of these insane sugar manufacturers. And I dare say any governments on neighbouring planets that they happen to have contacted.

The whole thing is a ghastly conspiracy. They carry on pumping sugar into us despite the fact that they know it rots our teeth, makes us fat, and finally kills us off completely.

And, worst of all, it induces severe states of paranoia.

The irony of it is that the body doesn't really need sugar at all. The Chinese, for instance, have an almost entirely sugar-free diet, and look how healthy they are . . . All right, they look a bit anaemic and yellow, but that's probably all that soy sauce and rice pudding.

Dairy Products

These are now acknowledged to be so bad for you that health-conscious Californians have been known to develop coronary problems at the sight of a plate of scrambled eggs.

Advertisers and the Milk Marketing Board do their best to give dairy products a healthy, natural image, and like to suggest that eggs, cream, milk and butter are a traditional part of the British diet.

Yet it is interesting to note that until relatively recently your average British family was too poor to afford dairy foods. This is because the average British worker was too ill to do much work, which in turn was because he lived mostly on what we now call health foods.

Milk

Different brands and how to identify them

Silver top = pasteurised
Red top = homogenised
Blue top = sterilised
No top = blue tits

However, all these are basically bad for you, and it's better to buy milk in cardboard cartons. Since these are more or less impossible to open, the milk inside does you no harm.

Meat and Poultry

'One man's meat is another man's poisson'
(Incompetent French translator)

It was with the correct version of these words that Nathaniel J. MacIntyre opened his now-famous fast food stall in Hicksville, Illinois, in 1898, calculating correctly that since Hicksville was full of restaurants selling perfectly good meat, one selling poisonous hamburgers would go down well.

(The hamburgers themselves didn't necessarily go down well, but that's another story.)

(There once was an ugly duckling . . . but that's another story as well.)

Meat, once thought to be the most nutritious of foods, is now on the condemned list along with the rest of them.

What it did to deserve this nobody knows. Certainly the animals themselves weren't consulted, and are now feeling thoroughly left out of things, rejected from society, unemployed etc.

In medical terms, meat is harmful because it is extremely fatty — especially red meat — and furthermore most of the fat is saturated; (polyunsaturated, as found in margarines, isn't so bad — and is also useful for filling in awkward cracks in plasterwork etc.).

Cakes and Biscuits

'Let them eat cake' is the most famous — and misunderstood — quotation about cakes in any hit record by Queen.

The original was by Marie Antoinette, and it was once thought to express her naïve ignorance of the fact that if the French peasants didn't have any bread,

they were hardly likely to keep a larder full of cakes.

Now, however, it is recognised as a cunning double entendre (or 'double meaning', as the French call it), meaning 'Don't let the peasants eat bread which is high in fibre, full of protein and generally rather good for them; let them eat cake which will rot their teeth, make them all diabetic and give them sugar-related weight problems.'

Cereals

Many manufacturers of breakfast cereals have jumped on the health-food bandwagon and produced cardboard boxes full of little bits of cardboard box, with appetising names like 'Dull Grey Bits', 'Crunchy Nuts and Bolts' and 'Sultana Gravel'.

Interestingly enough, cereals are the only food whose contents the average person is familiar with. This is because when you get bored reading about the special competition with a free trip to Florida for the sixth morning running, you turn the packet round and find to your horror that you're eating a mixture of 'Rolled oats, wheat bran, brown sugar, vegetable fat, bran, dried apple, hazelnuts, more bran, oat germ, salt, artificial flavouring, monosodium glutamate and bran etc.'

The normal reaction to this is to rush to the loo and throw up — hence the fact that cereals are considered an indispensable part of a calorie-controlled diet.

Vegetables

Vegetables are healthy, nutritious and altogether bursting with energy and goodness, and are not to be confused with vegetarians, who generally look pale, thin and rather ill.

Vegetarianism is the cult of avoiding meat, and it has some worrying side-effects. For instance, vegetarians are constantly complaining of aches and pains — usually as a result of being beaten up by owners of steak houses and hamburger joints.

The vegetarian justifies his stance on the basis of kindness to animals. However, a recent study has shown that the pig population of this country, which currently stands at 300,000, would drop to roughly 27 if nobody ate pork, ham or bacon.

Remember — vegetarians don't eat meat.

On the other hand, cannibals don't eat vegetarians.

Summary

To summarise, then, the perfect meal might consist of a couple of slices of wholemeal bread with a bowl of vegetable soup and some grilled fish, all washed down with unsweetened apple juice and breakfast cereal to follow.

Not an appetising prospect, admittedly, and a long way from the hearty, fattening feasts our grandparents enjoyed. In fact it's fair to say that their philosophy of four square meals a day with as much dairy food and sugar as possible is completely dead.

But what of our grandparents themselves? Unfortunately they're still alive . . . in fact they're coming for Christmas . . . must think of some excuse to go away this year . . .

Vitamins

It's always useful to know what effect different vitamins have, even though nobody can ever remember which foods they can actually be found in.

VITAMIN A Deficiency of vitamin A causes diminution of visual acuity in darkness. It also affects your eyesight.

Excess of vitamin A can have its problems, too. There is on record the case of a teenager who went on an all-carrot diet. After three months he became taller and abnormally thin. After six months his skin turned orange and his hair green. And then tragically . . . he got eaten by a giant rabbit.

VITAMIN B1 Deficiency of vitamin B1 causes beri-beri, a rare disease in which the victim repeats everything he says.

VITAMIN C Vitamin C is highly abundant in citrus fruits, fresh vegetables and small bottles of vitamin C tablets.

VITAMIN D Vitamin D deficiency causes rickets, a disease of bone formation.

The vitamin is contained in high proportions in fish oils, e.g. cod liver oil. The discovery of this vitamin has been of good service to man, though it has clearly done nothing for cod.

VITAMIN E Vitamin E is totally useless.

But scientists were so pleased with vitamins A, B, C and D they thought, what the hell?

Man doesn't need vitamin E.

The only thing it does is cause sterility in laboratory rats. Rats never eat it . . . unless forced to by scientists.

The Balanced Diet

As must surely be obvious from all that we have said, the most important thing is to make sure you have a properly balanced diet, otherwise you may end up suffering from one or other — perhaps both — of these extreme conditions:

OBESITY Often called the 'slimmer's disease', because it mostly affects people who are constantly slimming.

ANORAKSIA A pathological thinness and malnutrition caused by eating too many anoraks. Particularly vulnerable are impressionable teenagers and people who work in camping equipment stores.

At the time of writing there is still NO recorded case of this disease. For this we must thank not only the teams of doctors who have studied its causes, but also the anorak manufacturers who have tried to make their products taste as much like Kentucky Fried Chicken as possible to discourage people from eating them.

The Apple

● First came to prominence after a rather far-fetched story in which Eve, eager to pull the most eligible man around, took off all her clothes and proceeded to know him once in the Biblical sense and once in the bushes.

● Like most fruit, apples are high in vitamins — particularly *Vitamin C*. There is an old saying that 'An apple a day keeps the doctor away'. This is especially true if you throw it at him. (Another good way of keeping the doctor away is to poke an Armalite rifle through the letter-box at his crotch.)

● Apples are often associated with the meat of the pig. Roast pork is traditionally served with apple sauce. This fallacious habit stems from the days when farmers used to choke pigs to death by ramming apples down their throats.

● Granny Smith's, Cox's Pippin and Bramleys are among the most common names of English apples. Some of the least common are Deep Fried Tuna Chunks . . . Mavis Riley . . . the Pools Panel . . . Eric . . . and, of course, Chattanooga Choo-choos.

The Food Made Silly Problem Page

Ex-agony aunt of the *Daily Smut* Monica Stablightly has turned her wisdom and experience to problems in the kitchen. In this *Food Made Silly* exclusive, she answers some of our readers' culinary problems:

Dear Monica,

I can never get my cakes to rise. I use exactly the mixture as specified on the packet, and I keep opening the oven to see how they're getting on, but they always end up flat and soggy. Where am I going wrong?

Yours, Mrs D. Mulville, Clapham

Monica writes Many men go through this phase in middle age. Trying talking to your husband about his problem, or leading up to sex more gradually. Be sympathetic . . . be understanding . . . or in the final resort, give him a copy of Mayfair *to read.*

Dear Marge,

I can't tell you from butter.

Yours, C. Stewart, Northants

Monica writes Wrong newspaper. (see Glossary: Old Chestnuts)

Dear Monica,

I love meat and fish cooked in rich sauces, but it's so hard to make a white sauce which doesn't turn lumpy in the pan!

Yours, Exasperated, Lewisham

Monica writes For goodness sake — when will you learn that any intelligent man is more interested in your mind and your personality than in the size of your breasts? If he doesn't love you for what you really are then it's not worth the effort. Of course you could always wear falsies.

Dear Monica,

Since reading your fascinating book about food and fitness I have adopted a low-protein, low-fat diet in which I don't eat any meat, dairy products or vegetables. I must admit, it's taking a bit of getting used to — what do you think?

Yours, Mrs L. Perkins, Oxfordshire

Monica writes Sounds fascinating! Write to me again in a few weeks to let me know how you're getting on.

Dear Miss Stablightly,

It was kind of you to reply to my wife's letter about her new 'nothing' diet. I'm sure you'll be sorry to know that she died peacefully in her sleep three nights ago — she stuck to her diet to the very end, though.

Yours, Mr G. Perkins, Oxfordshire

Monica writes Full marks for determination!

Dear Miss Stablightly,

I note from our records that your current account is now £794.63 overdrawn, and would be grateful if you would take appropriate steps to rectify this situation as soon as possible.

Yours, J. Canter, Barclays Bank

Monica writes *This is probably a more common problem than you realise.*

Dear Monica:

I am a large Northern city. I think I'm far too big and sprawling.

Yours, Worried Manchester

Food and Etiquette

Many people worry about etiquette when invited out to dinner by friends. In the following pages we attempt to answer all your questions, so that when at a dinner party you can feel relaxed, enjoy the food, and successfully chat up the person sitting next to you.

Dinner Parties

(1) **Etiquette and manners are out of date, aren't they? So why should anyone worry about what to do?**

Well, it's certainly true that some forms of social behaviour have become much more relaxed in recent times, but it's important to remember that politeness and tact never go out of style, and observing basic standards and acceptable modes of deportment will ensure that you will feel at ease with your fellow human beings and avoid causing offence and embarrassment.

Any more questions, dick-head?

(2) **What are the basic Do's and Don't's?**

That's better. The basic 'Do's' and 'Don't's' are the lists of obvious things to do — or not to do — which break up the text in pointless magazine articles which tell people who are too ignorant to know any better than to read such trash how to behave.

(3) **Well, what are they in this case, then?**

Pretty obvious, actually. If you are invited out to dinner:

Do eat the food given to you.

Don't throw up all over your hostess if you dislike it.

Do bring a bottle of wine if you wish to make a contribution to the evening. (Even the richest host will appreciate such a gesture — it's probably how he became rich in the first place.)

Don't say 'Christ, I haven't got to drink this muck!' if your bottle is actually served to you.

Do give your hostess a polite kiss on leaving by way of thanks.

Don't put your hand up her skirt.

(4) **At a formal dinner or banquet, how do you know which cutlery to use for which course?**
Actually I don't want to be snobbish or anything, but you'd probably do better to keep away from smart dinners and banquets if you're going to use words like 'cutlery'.

For reasons you wouldn't understand — and I can't remember — we talk of knives and forks and spoons, but *never* cutlery.

But to answer your question, always start with the knife and fork set furthest away from you. With any luck this will mean that you eat the fish course with a fish knife and fork, the soup with a soup spoon etc. etc.

Though it will annoy the chap sitting at the far end of the table whose place setting you have raided.

(5) **Supposing my dinner party guests turn out to be a vegetarian who doesn't eat meat, a Jew who won't eat pork, a Hindu who won't eat beef, an Arab who won't eat if the Jew is there, an anorexic who won't eat, a slimmer, a reformed alcoholic, and a girl who nobody likes but who is married to the chap who brought the champagne? What should I do?**
Go out.

(6) **Should the ladies retire at the end of the meal?**
Most of them shouldn't have jobs in the first place! . . . No, seriously, that was a bit unnecessary . . . The business of

ladies retiring to another room is an old custom, and dates back to the days when it was laughably thought that men would want to discuss serious issues over a glass of port, while ladies would prefer each other's company so that they could natter on about knitting, embroidery and how good their husbands were in bed.

At modern dinner parties it's fair to assume that the women have all slept with each other's husbands, so the practice has been discontinued.

(7) **What about the conversation? What's the best approach to take?**

Many hosts and hostesses like to plan the conversation at their dinner parties in advance, rather like Robert Robinson on *Stop The Week* — only some hosts let their guests do the talking once in a while.

This certainly reduces the risk of getting on the subject of vegetarianism just as you serve up the Chateaubriand. Here is a basic guide (note the balance between 'light' and 'heavy' topics, which helps digestion):

Starter	Current industrial situation *or* sex
Fish course	Recent cult TV show *or* sex
Entrée	Terminal disease *or* sex
Dessert	'Who's sleeping with whom' *or* sex
Savoury	England's performance in Test Match *or* drugs
Cheese	World events, focusing on food shortages in East Africa *and* sex

The best way to shine or attract maximum attention at a dinner party is to make sure that the topic of conversation is always of your choice. One way to ensure this is to kill dead any topic started by someone else.

Here are some useful hints as to how you achieve this:

SOMEONE STARTS A CONVERSATION ABOUT . . .	AND YOU SAY . .
Skiing . . .	Oh, my parents were killed in a skiing accident . . .
Law. . .	Oh, my wife was killed in a legal accident . . . she fell down a loophole . . .
Mortgages . . .	It's very hard for orphans and one-parent families to get a mortgage . . .
Holidays . . .	I never go on holidays any more . . . not since the . . . er. . . plane crash . . .
Air-travel . . .	My parents were killed in a plane crash . . . it hit the mountain they were skiing down . . .

(8) **Finally, is it a good idea to dress for dinner?**
Yes.

Seating Plan for Dinner

(1) BAD

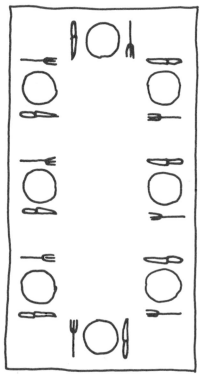

Jamie (host)

Hetherington
Master of Fox Hounds

Sally
Vegetarian teetotaller;
expert on plays of George
Bernard Shaw; has just split
up with Geoffrey after eight
meaningful years

Geoffrey
Alcoholic who saw Jamie
with Sarah

Roger
Double-glazing salesman
from Stanmore

Sarah
Who slept with Jamie last
night

Stig
The only Swede who
doesn't speak a word of
English

Louise (hostess)

(2) WORSE

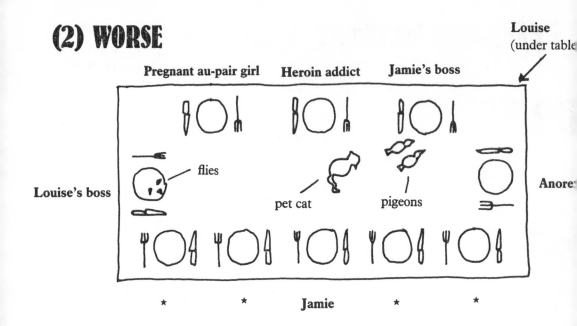

Pregnant au-pair girl   Heroin addict   Jamie's boss

Louise (under table)

Louise's boss

flies

pet cat   pigeons

Anorexi

★   ★   Jamie   ★   ★

★ Dagenham girl pipers

(3) WORST POSSIBLE

Local Restaurant

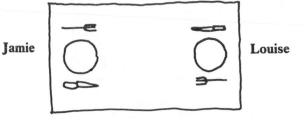

Jamie   Louise

Food and Sex

It was once thought by psychologists that there was a strong underlying link between food and sex.

This is because in the old days you generally had to take somebody out to dinner before you got the opportunity to sleep with them.

Nowadays this sort of thinking is seen as outmoded and offensive, so the subject is no longer seen as being of any interest at all.

Food Anxiety

Bewildered, puzzled and confused by all that you read about food? You may be suffering from a condition known as 'food anxiety'.

You're not the only one!

In fact, American scientists now say that the most common form of food-related disease is people who make themselves ill worrying about what they should and shouldn't eat.

DON'T WORRY!!

Recent research in a Cambridge laboratory by Nobel Prize-winning bore Professor C. J. Keightley has demonstrated that it can be proved that American scientists will say anything.

The A-Z of Meals

Dinner parties are of course a relatively recent invention. In pre-historic times, for instance, nobody had meals as such: primitive man just waited till he got hungry and then grabbed whatever came to hand.
Nowadays only single people living in bedsitters do this.
The rest of us like to formalise our eating habits, and as a result different names have been given to the different sorts of food we eat at different times of the day:

Afternoon tea

We all remember afternoon tea from our childhood. The rules were quite simple: you weren't allowed to get on to the cakes and gooey creamy things until you'd already stuffed yourselves full of sandwiches etc., by which time you'd completely lost your appetite.

Traditional features of children's tea parties include party hats, cardboard tubs of jelly, shortbread, and fat children who burst into tears for no reason.

Traditional features of adult tea parties include cucumber sandwiches, bone china cups and saucers, polite conversation, and fat adults who obviously went to too many children's tea parties.

Barbecue

Food that has been barbecued, as opposed to being grilled or fried, has a quite distinctive taste . . . a mixture of charcoal ash and paraffin.

Foods that are suitable for barbecues

include chops (lamb or pork), kebabs, sausages, spare ribs, corn on the cob, tomatoes, bacon etc.

Soup is distinctly ill-suited for the barbecue grill unless it is an extremely thick soup there's or an extremely thick chef.

Barbecues have a long and interesting history: they were once used by farmers as a way of ensuring instant and torrential rain.

Breakfast

The modern English breakfast — a bowl of muesli, a glass of orange juice and a quick glance through the *Guardian* — bears little resemblance to the substantial repast enjoyed by our forebears, who ate heartily and read a newspaper.

There was a time when breakfast consisted of several courses, and was regarded as one of the main meals of the day. Nowadays this sort of thing is only available on Inter-City connections by British Rail. You can have your porridge as you pull out of Euston, your kippers as you flash through Bedford, egg and bacon in the Yorkshire Dales, and a round of toast as you cross the border into Scotland.

You then remember that you were only going to Watford. So it's cost you an extra £69 for the ticket (plus £37.50 for the breakfast).

More recently eating breakfast has come to be seen as an indulgence, rather like lying in bed all morning. This can be shown most clearly by studying those 'Life in the day of . . .' columns in the colour supplements. The more rich, famous and successful the contributor is, the earlier they claim to get up, the further they claim to jog — and the less they claim to eat for breakfast.

But then lying probably made them rich, famous and successful in the first place.

Buffet

Just as a fondue (see *fondue*) is a meal laid on by a host who can't be bothered to cook, so a buffet is a meal laid on by a host who hasn't got any chairs. The word comes from the French for 'sideboard', which probably means he hasn't got a table either.

In fact there's almost nothing to be said for a buffet, unless you get a kick out of watching your guests trying to balance plates on their knees, looking for somewhere to put their wine glasses where they won't be kicked all over the carpet etc.

Like the barbecue (see *barbecue*), the word buffet is borrowed from the French . . . in the same way as we borrowed the Channel Islands . . . which they're not getting back either.

Christmas dinner

Christmas is a time when we spare a thought for those who are less fortunate than ourselves: the old, the sick, the lonely, the poor, and above all the hungry.

Then we get on with the real meaning of Christmas: roast turkey, potatoes, Brussels sprouts, plum pudding, brandy butter, mince pies and fruit cake, and falling asleep in front of the Queen (or if you're not lunching at Buckingham Palace — falling asleep in front of the telly).

Fondue

Fondues are very popular, except with the people who have to eat them, the people who have to prepare them, and everyone else.

In fact the 'fondue set' was invented purely to be given as a wedding present to someone you're indifferent to. There are two sorts available:

(1) *Cheese fondue*: a term invented by thrifty hosts who want to give their guests bread and cheese disguised as a complete meal.

(2) *Meat fondue*: really a cheese fondue, served to guests who you hope are too pissed to tell the difference.

Like barbecue sets, fondue sets

generally come with a selection of little two-pronged forks to stab your neighbour with. These forks usually have different coloured handles — so you can divide up into teams.

High tea

Idiomatic expression describing a certain sort of tea party enjoyed by hippies in the late 1960s and early 1970s (see *Magic Mushroom Omelette, Crazy Cookies, Acid Gingerbread* etc.).

Lunch

It has often been said, particularly by restaurant managers, that 'There is no such thing as a free lunch.'

Lunch means different things to different people. To manual workers from the Midlands, lunch means a pint of beer and a meat pie. To secretaries in London's West End, lunch means a hastily grabbed sandwich and a cup of coffee. To farm labourers in Upper Matabuliland who don't speak English, 'lunch' means 'sticking your head up a buffalo's arse'. So remember when you go there to be wary of any lunch invitations you get.

Not that lunch is a purely English phenomenon. The French are so keen on it that they start the day with a smaller version of it, 'le petit dejeuner', while we're still having breakfast (see *breakfast*). And the Italians and Spanish make such pigs of themselves over it that they have to lie down and sleep for the rest of the afternoon.

They call this the 'siesta'.

The nearest English equivalent is a job in advertising.

Luncheon

The meal before dinnereon.

Supper

When inviting guests, 'supper' is a useful word as it implies that you can't be bothered to make the full-blown effort you would if you were inviting them to 'dinner'.

People often talk about having a 'light supper before going to see a show'. What this actually means is that you order a meal at 7 o'clock, and at twenty-five past you're still waiting for it

to arrive, in the knowledge that the show begins in five minutes. Eventually it turns up, having sat on the counter for another three minutes waiting for the waitress to bring it to you, and you just manage a couple of mouthfuls before dashing for your seat . . . which unfortunately is facing the stage . . . and the play is so awful you spend the rest of the evening wishing you hadn't insisted on such snappy service.

Tea

An expression used by writers of modern television plays to indicate that they know perfectly well that working-class people never refer to 'supper' or 'dinner' (except when referring to lunch: see *lunch*).

Wedding breakfast

Like the working man's tea, which is in fact supper, the wedding breakfast is in fact lunch; unless the wedding is later in the day, in which case it may be tea or even dinner (and if the couple believe strongly in sex before marriage it may even become breakfast the next morning).

Wine and cheese party

A party at which you serve people either gin-and-tonics or cocktails, and feed them with crisps, peanuts, vol-au-vents, sausages and olives.

Macintyre's

In today's hectic, non-stop, all-systems-go world, with every-one rushing from appointment to meeting to rendezvous, it's not often that we get a chance to really spend time over lunch.

On those rare occasions when you're able to afford a full hour's lunch break —

Why not spend it standing in the queue of a MACINTYRE'S BURGER BAR waiting to be served?

MACINTYRE'S — WE PUT THE FASTING INTO FAST FOOD!!

Macintyre's — the Home of the Burger

Where to Buy Food

Supermarkets

Let's face it, there are advantages and disadvantages to shopping at supermarkets.

On the one hand the construction of large, purpose-built monstrosities on the edge of towns destroys local shops, empties city centres, and will eventually convert the whole of Britain into a poor man's version of one of the sleazier districts of Los Angeles, i.e. destroy civilisation as we know it.

On the other hand you can sometimes get a penny or two off a packet of sugar.

Going to a supermarket is sometimes described as 'one-stop shopping'. This is an odd term, as you have to *stop* in a traffic jam getting there (you have to go by car), *stop* to find a shopping trolley that goes in the direction you push it, *stop* to think where they might have hidden the washing-up liquid this week, *stop* for half an hour while the person in front of you unloads ten tons of shopping onto the wretched checkout girl, *stop* while the checkout girl has to ask the price of items without a label on, *stop* to find your cheque book when you realise you haven't got enough cash for all the extra things you were tempted to buy, *stop* in the queue to get out of the bloody car park, and then at the end of it all resolve to *stop* at home next time and send someone else.

Butchers, bakers, candlestick-makers (and grocers)

These are obsolescent terms for the type of shop that used to be found on every High Street.

Some still remain, and you should patronise them as much as possible by going in every day and saying 'my, my — what a lovely little butcher's shop you've got here.'

Bakers

Going to a baker's shop in this country is not a pleasurable experience. For some reason they are always staffed by a mixture of spotty, fat sixteen-year-old girls and wizened old women.

In either case they are dull souls who peer at you uncomprehendingly as you try to describe the type of bread or cakes you want to buy. Unless you are asking for something really simple, like a white loaf, always point at the things you want as if you were in a foreign country.

Also bear in mind that any nationally advertised bread is to be avoided. Only buy bread baked on the premises. Come to think of it, why not bake your own bread? Nothing beats the warm smell of your own freshly baked bread. In fact I think I'll come round and have some.

Fishmongers

Until very recently fish farming was impossible, as fish needed too much space to move around in, their dietary requirements were unknown and the tractors kept sinking to the bottom of the sea.

The fishmonger's shop, on the other hand, has been around for years, and is one of the delights of the British High Street.

Squeamish folk should not concern themselves too much with the live shellfish, such as crabs and lobsters, which have to be killed at home by plunging them in boiling water. Incredible as it may seem, crabs and lobsters actually *like* being boiled to death in this way. Certainly none has ever complained afterwards.

The fishmonger's shop will often double as a game seller: grouse, hares, pheasant, Monopoly etc. These again taste all the better for having been shot honourably on the wing, or in the leg, or through the whites of the eyes, rather than having been led like lambs to the slaughter (which is the case with pigs).

Delicatessens

'Delicatessen' is the German plural of a French word 'delicatesse' meaning 'nicety'. It is used to describe a shop run by Italians which sells cheese.

In fact delicatessens, which are increasingly popular, sell all the things that old-fashioned grocers' shops used to sell before they closed due to lack of demand.

Corner shops

When Pakistanis first came to this country they found it difficult to get paid employment because of difficulties with language, inexperience and any other excuse the management and unions could come up with.

This drove them to go into business in their own right, taking over thousands of corner shops, sub-post offices, off-licences etc. which they found would return a handsome profit by the simple expedient of staying open 22 hours a day every day of the year (except Christmas day — 24 hours).

When it was first coined, the term 'Paki shop' had a twinge of racial abuse to it, but this was lost as the characteristics of the Paki shop as opposed to the old-fashioned British shop became apparent, i.e. the former is open any time you want to shop and sells as many things as possible whereas the latter closes at 5.30 p.m. or before, never opens Sunday, has half-day closing when you least expect it and tries to stock as narrow a range as it can.

'Paki shop' now means any shop that meets its customers' requirements and can in fact be run by Pakistanis, Indians, Greeks, Turks, Italians, Cypriots or anyone of any nationality, even, in theory (but rarely in practice), a native Englishman.

Beans

Beans are among the healthiest foods we eat and come in a wide variety of forms:

(1) **Baked beans** — the ones that make you fart

(2) **Aduki beans** — Japanese beans that make you fart

(3) **Runner beans** — beans that make you think you're going to fart, then you realise it's something else and have to do a runner to the lavatory

(4) **Kidney beans** — so-called because of their shape

(5) **French beans** — so-called because of their accent

(6) **Chilli beans** — so-called because they are most often found in tins marked 'chilli beans'

(7) **Has beens** — so-called because they appear on the Des O'Connor Show.

!!Shop Cockney!!

Depressed by all those faceless, impersonal, convenient, low-priced supermarkets?

Why not 'SHOP COCKNEY' and get your groceries from your local fruit'n'veg man? He's sure to:

- Chat to the person ahead of you in the queue while you freeze to death

- Call you 'Me ol' darlin'' in a phoney accent

- Give you more than you asked for — and charge for it

- Shovel unwashed potatoes into your smart new shopping bag

!!SHOP COCKNEY!!

AS RECOMMENDED BY BENNY GREEN, DEREK JAMESON AND ALL THE REST OF THEM . . .

Types of bread

(1) **White tin loaf** The ordinary 'large white loaf' or 'small white loaf' (depending on its size). It is called a 'tin loaf' because it has no heart and tastes as if it's full of preservatives . . . which it probably is.

(2) **Wholemeal loaf** White bread is made from refined grain. In wholemeal bread unrefined grain, chaff, stems, roots, bits of old fertiliser bags, farmer's lung etc. are used giving the loaf its characteristically healthy, nutbrown, chewy and foul-tasting properties.

(3) **French loaf** Any English bread, however unlike the taste of real French bread, which has the shape of General de Gaulle's nose.

(4) **French stick** Any implement a Frenchman is tempted to use to beat an English baker for daring to call his bread 'French'.

(5) **French kiss** Rather like so-called French bread, i.e. you don't know till afterwards whether it will leave a nice or nasty taste in the mouth.

(6) **Bridge rolls** Like ordinary rolls, only each person gets given 13 at the beginning (hence 'Baker's dozen').

(7) **Bath Bun** (see Sponge)

(8) **Brown bread** Cockney rhyming slang for dead; as in expressions such as:
> 'This brown bread's been poisoned.'
> *or*
> 'How did he die, Constable?'
> 'A bit of brown bread stuck in his throat, sir.'

With the enormous variety of cheeses available on the market it's very difficult to remember which is which. This unique guide helps you to identify different brands by smell.

Types of cheese

CHEESE

Cheshire   Has a bland but fresh and rounded aroma preferred by those who like a mild cheese.

Caerphilly   Fullbodied and rich though without the pungency of blue cheeses.

Double Gloucester   Reminiscent of the English countryside, mellow and warm.

Babybel   Musty and a mite repellent.

Derby   A nose-wrinkling, bowel-loosening tang.

Appenzell   The changing rooms of the Arsenal–Tottenham game at half-time.

Camembert   Smells like a piece of Brie removed by health inspectors from a Turkish bath just off the Portobello Road.

Emmenthal   Redolent of the inside of a public phone box during a heatwave.

Danish Blue	Smells like a body found in Epping forest by schoolkids, obviously murdered about a month ago.
Lymeswold	Reeks of media hype.
Stilton	The hamster cage you'd forgotten about before you went on your three-week holiday.
Sage Derby	A soiled contraceptive filled with herbal shampoo.

Grimedale

In the seven-year-old tradition of Lymeswold and Melbury comes a distinctively British cheese, Grimedale.

With the creamy consistency of lard, the crunchy texture of gravel, and dotted with tiny flecks of blue asbestos, the taste of Grimedale will put you in mind of the bleak, windswept landscapes of the industrial North.

At £4.95 a pound it's got to be the housewives' choice.

GRIMEDALE

— a dour cheese from the land of Black Pudding and unemployment.

Buying Beef

Why are they sticking needles into me?

Indicators

Double Top

Horn

Leatherhead

Centre of Birmingham

Bull's Eye

Bull's neck

Montana

North Dakota

Baron of Beef

Sirloin of Steak

Cocktail Stick

Lord Aberdeen of Angus

Rump (1653)

Electric Fence

Spare Ribs

Gay News

Cow Slip

Arrow

Shin Pad

Offal

Dreadful

Ox Tail

Oxtail soup

Map of Italy

Odd Socks

Beef Wellington

Bullshit

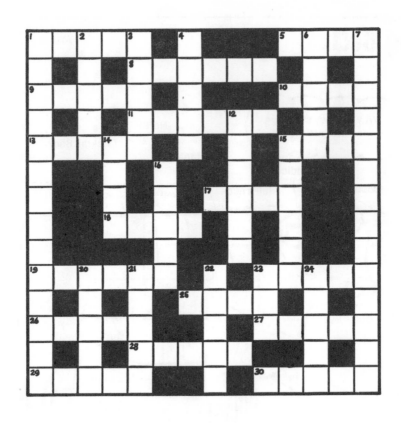

Food Made Silly Crossword

And now it's time to exercise the old grey matter . . . or porridge as they call it in Scotland.

THE FOOD MADE SILLY CRYPTIC CROSSWORD.

Crossword fans will be captivated by the challenge of the Made Silly Crossword which actually features some of the blank squares from the more difficult crosswords in *The Times*. Some of the clues and answers are concerned with food and drink. But not all. And some of the answers are even spelled correctly.

Doc. O'Klug! (anag.)

Across

1/ Refined foodstuff we hear you might find in the garden. (5)
5/ A common English dish from Italy served with bol. (4)
8/ The first thing you must do with truffles before eating. (6)
9/ Readers of this book, ignited between the same point. (5)
10/ German name similar to Rosie. (4)
11/ Pointless captain fish. (6)
13/ It is a piece of cake when you take it from a youngster? (5)
15/ Peat cooking is a French speciality. (4)
17/ Drink adds point to a victory. (4)
18/ Is the animal wild because it has a bad leg? (4)
19/ Fish found in nasal monster. (6)
23/ Short day always means something meaty to eat in Indonesia. (5)
25/ Rearrange loop so there's a hole in the middle. (4)
26/ Top o' the cake, to you! (5)
27/ Ear of corn stars. (5)
28/ Chasm in America by boat. (5)
29/ Three-pointer is a signal to go. (5)
30/ Warm up tungsten first to get corn. (5)

Down

1/ Habillement. (6, 8)
2/ Many a tear shed over this. (5)
3/ Smokie . . . but not Arbroath. (5)
4/ Food for poker. (5)
6/ Bread said to be rock. (5)
7/ Common girl left on her own becomes sweet. (10, 4)
12/ The finish comes before I have this chicory. (6)
14/ Lies in a field and sounds like a bell. (4)
15/ Continental sea-food dish made by removing small part of knee cap. (6)
16/ Melon gone off. (5)
20/ French law concerning wine-growing district. (5)
21/ Nothing removed from this pointless herb makes instrument. (5)
22/ Lady Astor makes Sunday lunch. (5)
23/ Letters sent on Mayday? (3)
24/ This food is rubbish! (5)

*Solution on p. 96

Back to the Fegato Verde at last! Franco met me at the door with a smile which immediately told me that my cheque had bounced last time. My companion, who I shall refer to as John for personal reasons (and because his real name is Oswald Nodick and he gets embarrassed about it) settled up for me and we went in.

'Put on a little weight, signorina?' said Franco cheekily as he and three waiters struggled with a crowbar to get me through the doorway. The decor at the Fegato Verde was, as always, subtly but quintessentially Italian . . . fourteen colour photos of the Juventus team, an easy-to-follow 1982 World Cup chart and a life-size photo of Sophia Loren in a swimsuit signed personally by Trevor Francis (Sampdoria and England).

Romano the young waiter showed us to our table, lit the candle and groped off to put another 50p in the electricity meter.

Saturday night, Sunday night, Monday night, Tuesday

'Restaurant of the Year'

night, Wednesday night, Thursday night or Friday night. I knew instinctively that it was going to be one of those nights. Inebriated with the romance of the surroundings John kissed me on the cheek. I turned round, lowered my dress and sat down.

The aperitifs arrived promptly. John had ordered a small lager and I, a Campari and soda. We both felt the new barman had overdone the Campari . . . a large measure was perhaps OK for my Campari and soda but a little excessive in the small lager.

The Fegato Verde offer a wide variety of hors d'œuvres. John plumped for the seafood cocktail and I went for my favourite, the prosciutto e melone. They were both superbly scrumptious. John kept trying to pinch my melon and I kept trying to grab his winkle. This distracted the waiters while he felt my tit and I fondled his tool.

The barman came over with the wine list. We asked for something light, cool and crisp and he brought us a cucumber.

It was at this point that a large black limousine drew up outside and two men brandishing machine guns burst in and mowed down the family of four at the next table. It's this attention to detail that makes the Fegato Verde so quaintly Italian.

For our main course I chose the pollo sorpressa — chicken breast rolled, breaded and stuffed with cheese, herbs and garlic butter — and John went for the rognoncini trifolati (kidneys in red wine sauce cut into delicate leaf-like shapes). Time for some more wine. To make it easier for the inexperienced barman we just pointed to no. 27 on the list and he promptly brought us a portion of special fried rice.

The pollo sorpressa was divinely garlicky. 'I won't have to worry about vampires tonight!' I quipped. John was deeply offended. He *is* a vampire, you see, and is highly sensitive about things like that. (I'll never forget the time we went to a Berni's and I ordered a wooden steak . . . but I digress.)

We kissed and made up . . . he looked much better with a bit of make-up on.

To add to the atmosphere of heavenly romance Giampero the head waiter wandered around from table to table playing the violin. He stopped by our table and stared at me lovingly. He had an ear for music . . . an eye for the ladies . . . and a kidney for medical research. With the music and wine I felt entranced as if under some exotic gipsy spell. Something welled up inside me . . . was it love? . . . was it desire? . . . was it lust? No, it was the pollo sorpressa . . . coming back for another sorpressa.

I rushed to the powder room trying to maintain some dignity. I hope I hadn't embarrassed John. He was too much of a gentleman to mention the copious beige-coloured vomit that had gone all over his head. Thank heavens he was bald, I thought.

A little apprehensively I returned to the restaurant . . . no one had noticed, I'm glad to say. Everything was back to normal. Giampero had put down his gipsy fiddle and was now going round each table selling clothes-pegs.

The bill came and I was reminded what excellent value the Fegato Verde is. Starter, main course, dessert, aperitif, two bottles of wine, coffee and brandy came to a mere £48.50. So we added a tennis racquet — for Romano's service.

As John and I are old friends we decided to go dutch. So we both paid 10 guilders and ran for it!

Your Starter for Ten

Now that you have read our book perhaps you'd like to take this opportunity to test your general food knowledge and see how many interesting facts you've picked up. (*Answers on page 84.*)

(1) Look carefully at this list of typical ingredients for a traditional Sunday lunch. Which one doesn't quite fit?

        Roast beef
        Yorkshire pudding
        Roast potatoes
        Cement
        Gravy
        Brinjal Bhaji

(2) Where might you bite someone's 'knackers' and what would happen to you if you did?

(3) In not more than six words name your ten favourite Chinese dishes. (It can be done!)

(4) (Italian teaser) 'Lasagne verdi' . . . Do you . . . Eat it? Listen to it at the Royal Opera House? Wear it?

(5) Which foodstuff is associated with the 4th Earl of Sandwich (1718–92)?

(6) Which popular children's tea party speciality is a former Labour peer?

          Is it . . .   (a) A blancmange?

                              (b) Iced tea-cakes?

                              (c) Chocolate ice-cream?

                              (d) Sausage rolls?

        Beware – this is a trick question

(7) Which one of the following three is out of place?

          (i) Peking Duck

          (ii) Bombay Duck

          (iii) Aylesbury Bus Station

(8) From which creature do we get . . .

        Sweetbreads?

        Tripe?

        Bull's bollocks?

(9) From which country do we get . . .

        (a) Apfelstrudel?

        (b) Satay?

        (c) VD?

        (d) Arnavot cigeri?

        (e) Turkey?

(10) (Fruity question)

What did Nell Gwynn sell?

Your Starter for Ten Answers

(1) Cement. Brinjal Bhaji is of course an integral part of Sunday lunch in India.

(2) Germany. A knacker is a spicy German sausage.

(3) Nos. 12–19, 45 and 78.

(4) All three. It is a very pleasant form of pasta. You can listen to it at the Royal Opera House but you won't hear much over the din of those rowdy opera singers. And you can wear it: you can cover yourself all over with lasagne and go to a fancy dress party as a silly tit.

(5) The Wellington Boot. Lord Sandwich was a compulsive gambler and refused to leave the gaming tables even to eat. So in order not to starve to death he began eating his Wellington boots . . . hence the 'sandwich'. (See also Balaclava helmet, Raglan sleeve, Leotard etc.)

(6) Aston Villa. They beat Rotherham United.

(7) Bombay duck. It is in fact a small fish of the salmon family, dried and salted and eaten as a relish. The other two aren't fish at all.

(8) A butcher.

(9) (a) Austria

  (b) Indonesia et al.

  (c) Any country . . . depends which airline you use.

  (d) Turkey.

  (e) Arnavot cigeri.

(10) No marks for guessing the answer to this question. (We'll also accept 'oranges'.)

Glossary

A la carte   On menus, as distinct from table d'hôte . . . the Chef's special . . . à la carte signifies food that has fallen off the back of a lorry.

Aberdeen Angus   (a) A breed of cattle (b) A particularly tough yobbo who works for a chain of bookies in Glasgow . . . will go to any lengths to recoup outstanding gambling debts.

There is a story of a tiny drunken tramp who arrives at the gates of heaven to be greeted by St Peter's keen displeasure.
'We can't let you in here, you're a tramp. We only let the great in here.'
'But I am great,' protests the tramp. 'I once called Aberdeen Angus a poof!'
'When was that?' asks St Peter.
'Oh, about ten seconds ago.'

Anchovy   A small but deadly fish related to the herring family . . . though I saw the Herring family at Christmas and they strongly deny this.

Apple   Sir Isaac Newton is said to have been sitting underneath an apple tree when a banana fell on his head . . . and he discovered the laws of cross-pollination.

Artichoke   A rather interesting upper-middle class pre-prandial game invented by Rubric. Each participant is given an 'artichoke' which is a small ball consisting of green, fibrous wood shavings stuck together over the central 'heart'. The idea of the game is to remove all the woody bits (bowls of melted butter are provided to make this slightly easier) and try to find some part of the artichoke which is edible.

Avocado   A Spanish lawyer. Noted for the oily green colour, the soft exterior concealing a hard inside. They can be bought quite easily . . . using cash and preferably used notes.

Bacon   'Bacon and eggs must be the greatest British invention'

Shakespeare

'Shakespeare and eggs must be the greatest British invention'   *Bacon*

Bamboo shoots   Not as popular as they once were. People tend to prefer shooting pheasant, grouse, or even deer nowadays, all of which make for better sport.

Bananas   The same as nuts. As in the expression 'He drove me bananas!'

Bass   A European fish of the perch family. There are two main sorts of bass: (a) *The gut-bass*, which is stretched from an old broom and stuck in a tea-chest; (b) *the electric bass*, which is hung round the neck and plugged into an amplifier.

(NB The electric bass should not be confused with the electric eel — a dangerous sea-snake. There is also an acoustic eel, which is preferred by beginners and folk-singers.)

Beef   Beef is one of the most versatile of the popular meats . . . it can sing, juggle, do impressions and breakdance.

Beetroot (see also *sugarbeet*, *Merseybeat* and *Jack Kerouac*)   This amusing vegetable can always be relied upon, at boring dinner parties, to discolour the guests' faeces and urine. It is one of Russia's most popular vegetables — one of their national dishes is a form of beetroot soup called 'bortsch'. Hardly surprising the beetroot is so popular with the Ruskies . . . in so drab, dreary and humourless a country a bright purple turd or red piss must seem like damned fine comedy.

Brains   Unfortunately what is true of liver (i.e. eating liver is good for your liver) is not true of brains (calf's or sheep's). Eating brains does not improve your intelligence. And sadly it is also not true of other things. I speak as a man who has spent months eating stallion pricks.

Broccoli   More than one Broccolo.

Cannelloni   Usually stuffed with cream cheese or minced meat, this white, pasty, hollow, tube-like Italian painter lived from 1697 to 1768, which I think is plenty. He is best remembered by 250-year-old Venetians with good memories.

Capers   Pickled rat turds. Put by French chefs into English salads out of sheer historical enmity.

Caviar   The unborn children of the sturgeon fish. Black, oily, gritty and revolting, it has all the hallmarks of a delicacy. The Tsars of Russia were particularly fond of caviar until they got slaughtered by peasants and lefties . . . then they rather went off it.

Chestnuts   There are three sorts:
(1) *Horse chestnuts*
(2) *Sweet chestnuts*
(3) *Old chestnuts* . . . like this one:
A landlady has three lodgers all of whom are keen football enthusiasts. At Sunday lunch she is about to carve the chicken when she asks one of the young men which football team he supports.

'Tottenham Hotspur,' replies the lad. 'Well I'll give you the chicken wings, then,' says the landlady, 'because Spurs are very good on the wing at the moment.'
Then she asks the second man which team he supports.
'Manchester United,' he replies.
'Then you shall get the middle of the breast, because United have a very good midfield this season.'
Then she asks the third one which team he supports. He replies quickly, 'Crystal Palace . . . but I'm not hungry.'

Chicken   Probably the most popular and versatile meat in the world, the chicken has achieved this universal acclaim due to one unique feature — its major internal organs are all located in a vacuum-wrapped plastic bag.

Christmas cake   A rich dark fruit cake which is protected from being eaten by several layers of marzipan and rock-hard icing sugar. It is usually made at least two months before Christmas and thrown away intact in early February.

Christmas pudding   A large, heavy, stodgy concoction traditionally consumed by people who have eaten too much already but are too polite to say 'no'. (**Boxing Day pudding** Same as Christmas pudding only the cream has begun to go off.)

Coconut Nature's way of storing empty space.

Cod Along with chips, the most important ingredient of cod and chips. The head of the cod can be boiled to make fish stock or tied around the waist and suspended over the genitalia. It has religious associations and was much revered in the Bible. 'The piece of Cod which passeth all understanding . . .' St Paul's epistle to the Chippies.

Corn (See most of this book.)

Corn on the cob Another excuse for eating lots of melted butter (see *artichoke*, *asparagus* etc.). Interestingly enough, it takes a man with only one tooth seventeen days to eat a corn on the cob.

Convenience food Technical term for food that smells as if it's been prepared in a Gent's lavatory (see also *cottage cheese*).

Cranberries Berries from a cran.

Croissants Similar to 'croûtons', 'croissants' is French for 'balls', as in the phrase: 'Croissants! Pourquoi n'avons-nous pas le petit déjeuner anglais?' (translation: 'Oh balls! Why can't we have egg and bacon for breakfast like the English?')

Croûtons French word for 'bollocks!' made famous by the celebrated chef of the court of Louis XIV who was reputed to have exclaimed one day in the kitchens, 'Croûtons! J'ai laissé tomber dans le potage quelques morceaux de pain frit!' (translation: 'Bollocks! I've dropped some bits of fried bread in the soup!')

Crumpet This perfectly respectable English word has fallen into the hands of the smutty, prurient filthmongers who have completely changed its meaning so that you can hardly use the word any more without people thinking of a soft, unsweetened griddle cake, toasted and served with butter.

Cucumber A gherkin that's showing off.

Food and the Royals

Would you believe that, despite all the magnificent twelve-course banquets she attends, the Queen's favourite way of spending an evening is to curl up in front of the telly with a plate of scrambled eggs and watch a video of the Grand National?

You'd believe anything, wouldn't you?

Or that King George V — no stranger to 'haute cuisine' — enjoyed the Dish of the Day at Pat's Café in Dagenham before he died . . . ? Just before he died, as a matter of fact.

You'll find these and many other fascinating facts in a new, lavishly illustrated book, *Food and the Royals*.

● What is Princess Di's special recipe for tuna fish salad?

● Does she breastfeed the children in front of the servants?

● Does she breastfeed the servants in front of the children?

Food and the Royals: probably the most fatuous load of rubbish yet published about the dull old Windsors.

!!IN YOUR BOOKSHOPS NOW !!

REMAINDERED FOR HALF THE PRICE NEXT MONTH!!

The Joy of Dripping

Caroline Thistlethwaite

A companion volume to Caroline Thistlethwaite's highly successful *The Little Lard Book*, *The Joy of Dripping* takes a frank, down-to-earth look at dripping and the role it plays in people's lives. Plus handy recipes, useful cooking tips and half-a-dozen tasteful illustrations.

Dogfish   One of the few fishes that pisses against a lamp post.

East Grinstead   Not a food at all, but a small town in Kent not far from Tunbridge Wells. It does, however, boast an excellent little restaurant, I can't quite remember where . . . oh, yes, 47 Church Street . . . called La Dauphinoise, which quite coincidentally is run by my brother.

Fish and finger pie   A phrase used in a Beatles song believed by those in the know to have something to do with sex (see *Sex Made Silly*).

Fish fingers   A long-term fraud practised on the public who still haven't woken up to the fact that fish do not have fingers.

Flounder (verb intrans.)   To stumble awkwardly due to having two flat fish strapped to your feet.

Frog's legs   A French delicacy tasting, to the educated palate, like old chicken wings boiled in swimming-pool water. Much sought after by lame frogs.

Gammon   Bacon that has had things added to its price.

Garlic   A pungent little vegetable, not unlike an onion, used to flavour meat, stews, French underground trains etc. Said to keep vampires away . . . hence Dracula's decision to travel by taxi while in Paris.

Garlic press   A newspaper distributed free to all those concerned with the cultivation, sale and supply of garlic in the UK and overseas.

Ginger   Cockney rhyming slang for 'queer' (i.e. homosexual) from 'ginger beer'. Used in such expressions as 'give us a pint of ginger beer, you great poof!'

Gooseberries   The very rare berries found growing on geese. The gooseberry is a particularly bitter and acid fruit, and has come to mean any person who is excluded from a group or couple because he or she is hairy with green veins.

Grouse (verb intrans.)   To whine or complain . . . particularly about being shot in mid-flight by upper-class wallies.

Haggis A convenience food. Convenient that is for Scots who want to get rid of any old rubbish or left-overs lying about the kitchen (mincemeat, oatmeal, offal, heather, shredded kilt, broken bottles, razor blades, old photos of money etc.). These ingredients are stuffed into a sheep's bladder (preferably with the sheep removed) which is then boiled until New Year's Eve, when it is kicked through your neighbour's window for three points.

Hake, Haddock and Halibut A firm of solicitors.

Hot dog A tasty frankfurter sold in cinema foyers which, despite its name, is not made from dog meat (in this sense rather like **Shepherd's pie** . . . which isn't made from dog meat either, though it often tastes that way).

Jerusalem artichoke The Jerusalem artichoke is a very waggish plant indeed, the arch conman of the vegetable world. It is not an artichoke and it has nothing to do with Jerusalem. I think we're all agreed that this is a very droll wheeze indeed — never again will it be said that sunflowers don't have a sense of humour.

Kidney So called because it's the same shape as a kidney bean.

Kipper A large ungulated pachyderm of Africa and Southern Asia characterised by one or two horns on its nose. It can be very dangerous and has been known to charge at Land-Rovers knocking them over and goring their inhabitants to a grisly death. Well, come on! If you don't know what a kipper is . . . !

Lamb An English essayist with a silent 'b'. (He also had a silent 'p' he achieved by lagging his bog with polystryene tiles.)

Lobster Like crab, this is a vastly overrated seafood which to be enjoyed fully needs great physical strength, prodigious will-power and a sundry assortment of metal implements used in former times for torturing infidels.

Mackerel Popular fish abundant in our coastal waters. It is often available vacuum-wrapped in thick plastic, when it is called a packamackerel.

Meringue Basically this is egg white

and icing sugar whipped long enough for it to be misspelt (see **Baked Alasker**).

Meringue-utan A hairy brown tree-dwelling dessert found in Malaysia.

Mint An aromatic green herb extracted from toothpaste.

Mint sauce Replacing the pound note with an unsightly coin.

Muesli Once described by trendy food faddists to be the best thing to have come out of Switzerland since sliced bread, until they remembered that they didn't like sliced bread and it didn't come from Switzerland anyway.

Measly Like muesli only comes in smaller portions.

Oyster Nose-bogey and sea-water served in a natural ash-tray.

Ploughman's lunch French bread, cheddar cheese and brown chutney — invented to mark the disappearance of the last actual ploughman in the country, and served at lunchtime in pubs.

Pigs Some people have very strong views indeed about the eating of pig flesh. Some pigs also have strong views on this subject but they are largely ignored in this piggist society in which we live. Jewish people remove all bacon and pork from their fridges and hide it under the stairs when their mothers call round unexpectedly.

Ploughman's breakfast An enormous meal to make up for the fact that there is only bread and cheese for the rest of the day.

Rock salmon Dogfish (see *dogfish*).

Shark Someone who sells dogfish and calls it salmon.

Sodium chloride Salt.

Sodium bloody chloride Common salt.

Stuffed aubergine (see *Stewed apple*, *Jugged hare*, *Canned pineapple* and *Slightly tipsy rhubarb*.)

Swede A Scandinavian who believes in free love, weekend prison and kagools. In Scotland, a *turnip*.

Welsh rarebit   The highpoint of Welsh culinary tradition (sic).

Yarmouth Bloaters   If Yarmouth is famous for anything, then it must be for its bloaters. Ever heard of Yarmouth bloaters? Oh . . . in that case, Yarmouth isn't famous for anything. A bloater is a small herring which is partially dried and smoked. Scholars at Eton, not noted for their high intelligence, put on stripey blazers in the summer and wear bloaters on their heads.

Answers

Across: 1/Flour 5/Spag. 8/Exhume 9/Elite
10/Otto 11/Kipper 13/Candy 15/Pate 17/Wine
18/Game 19/Salmon 23/Satay 25/Polo 26/Icing
27/Spica 28/Abyss 29/Green 30/Wheat

Down: 1/French dressing 2/Onion 3/Reeky 4/Chips
6/Pitta 7/Gooseberry tart 12/Endive 14/Dung
15/Paella 16/Lemon 20/Loire 21/Organ 22/Roast
23/SOS 24/Tripe